The Arkansas Testament

THE
ARKANSAS
TESTAMENT
DEREK WALCOTT

The Noonday Press

Farrar, Straus and Giroux

New York

Published in Canada by Harper & Collins, Toronto
Printed in the United States of America
Designed by Cynthia Krupat
First edition, 1987
Second printing, 1990
Library of Congress Cataloging-in-Publication Data
Walcott, Derek.
The Arkansas testament.
I. Title.
PR9272.9.W3A85   1987   811   87-323

Acknowledgments are made to *The Atlantic*, *The Graham House Review*,
The Literary Review, *The New Republic*, *The New York Review of Books*,
The Paris Review, *Parnassus*, *The Partisan Review*, *Pequod*, *PN Review*
(London), *River Styx*, and *TriQuarterly*, where some of these poems originally
appeared. "Marina Tsvetaeva" and "Storm Figure" appeared originally
in *Antaeus*; "The Lighthouse" and "Fame" appeared originally in
The New Yorker—all in slightly different form.

For Seamus Heaney

Contents

HERE

ELSEWHERE

HERE

The Lighthouse

Under his photographer's shroud,
the mountain facing our town
focussed the sunset, pressed a cord—
all the street lamps flashed on.

I swivel his creaking set
of postcards fifty years later:
the lighthouse, a silhouette
of sloops on fiery water.

Stars pierce their identical spots
over Castries; they repeat
those to-be-connected dots
in a child's book, which I complete

lamp by lamp up to La Place.
A night with white rum on its breath
walks with me at funeral pace
to lengthen the town. Underneath

the market's arc lamp, a crowd
is heckling some speaker. A face
peers at me, then loosens its screwed
squint. Shouts. The hand-pumping farce

of old times! From the headland,
briefly catching the gusty wicks
of black sea grapes, the minute hand
of the luminous dial sticks

at the New Jerusalem Bar.
I order a flask of Old Oak.
The crowd follows a different star
now, but with an old patois joke

he unscrews the cap with a squint,
then gargles the politician's
harangue. In no time, I'm bent
double with laughter. Once,

he could lift hysterical fans
on the hook of an eyebrow. Their noise
is now for the speaker. Black hands
in a corner slap down dominos.

Wiping wet eyes with wet palms,
aching from all those distraught
recollections in double rums,
we split up on the dark street.

I to the black promontory
of Vigie, the dots sprinkled on
in its villas. He to a glori-
ous piss, and a sleep. A full moon

rose at the end of the road,
minting the harbour with scales.
A coin, tossed once overhead,
that stuck there, not heads or tails.

The road, held up to its light
would show, like a negative,
the days I walked there; I recite
to that zero all I believe.

By the airport, across dim grave-
stones, the seraphic beam revolves
its white lance. Shawled waves
spread the lace of altar cloths.

From wayside bushes, a girl's
laughter. A lit shack. Your kerosene
lamp, Philomene, that a Bible's
thin pages of calico screen.

Unaging moonlight falls
on the graves; penknives of grass
incise other initials
on scarred desks that were ours.

But he, that lovely actor
lost in the post office! Stripped.
A superfluous character
written out of the script.

Apart from one trip abroad,
he stayed here fifty years. Fifty.
He moves with his island, the blade
of the lighthouse dips in the sea.

So, when some street lamp echoed
our ring of boys breaking up,
was the moon, rolled from its cloud,
the dice in a gambler's cup

that sent him home to a boy's
daydreams on a crowded bed?
Tonight I laughed at the voice,
not the graying, socketed head.

Does any pattern connect
the domino dots of these stars
with the black slabs ranged erect
in the palms of those gamblers?

In my room, the air conditioner's
freezing. It drips. Its racked hum
excludes you, Philomene, and the stars
in your coal pot. The heat of home.

As soon as its noise rattles off,
the surf, or a frenzy of palms,
hisses, "You had losses. Enough.
You can't hold them all in your arms.

"For more care in the craft of verse,
kneel, for the sand's moonlit linen.
For hills that ignore the moon's curse
and sleep with their window open.

"Sleep, sleep. Tomorrow, the dread
of what may drop out of the blue."
I cannot, the levelling blade
flashes on faces I knew.

The house where we used to live,
its vine-twined verandah gone,
is a printery now; not a leaf
will curl from its pillars again.

II

Morning. Light-fingered shade. A red door,
chipped basins under a pipe,

and, from its brass crown, water
plaiting in a white whip.

Young Rastas lean in a yard.
A rooster, safe, struts in the sun.
A red-green-and-yellow board
crows: MAN IS A BABYLON.

At noon, down a crooked street,
children run screaming from school.
Some fall. Some will take the straight
road from their galvanized hell.

Then, far as that crackling noise
of a boyhood climbing the wind,
the kites of breadfruit leaves rise
from the dry yard of my mind,

as a breeze creases the sea,
shadowing the breadfruit's bark,
and brightens with January
the harbor facing La Toc.

III

The ghost of the lighthouse will sleep
all day like an actor. A song
pins sheets on a line. A white ship
carries others where they belong,

as I watch a low seagull race
its own cry, like a squeaking pin
from the postcard canoes of La Place,
where the dots I finished begin,

and a vendor smiles: "Fifty? Then
you love home harder than youth!"
Like the full moon in daylight, her thin,
uncontradictable truth.

Cul de Sac Valley

A panel of sunrise
on a hillside shop
gave these stanzas
their stilted shape.

If my craft is blest;
if this hand is as
accurate, as honest
as their carpenter's,

every frame, intent
on its angles, would
echo this settlement
of unpainted wood

as consonants scroll
off my shaving plane
in the fragrant Creole
of their native grain;

from a trestle bench
they'd curl at my foot,
C's, R's, with a French
or West African root

from a dialect throng-
ing, its leaves unread
yet light on the tongue
of their native road;

but drawing towards
my pegged-out twine
with bevelled boards
of unpainted pine,

like muttering shale,
exhaling trees refresh
memory with their smell:
bois canot, bois campêche,

hissing: *What you wish*
from us will never be,
your words is English,
is a different tree.

II

In the rivulet's gravel
light gutturals begin,
in the valley, a mongrel,
a black vowel barking,

sends up fading ovals;
by a red iron bridge,
menders with shovels
scrape bubbling pitch,

every grating squeak
reaching this height
a tongue they speak
in, but cannot write.

Like the lost idea
of the visible soul

still kindled here
on illiterate soil,

blue smoke climbs far
up, its vein unveering,
from that ochre scar
of a charcoal clearing.

Crusted clouds open
like the pith of loaves
in a charred clay oven
wrapped in fig leaves.

In a rain barrel, water
unwrinkles to glass;
a lime tree's daughter
there studies her face.

The sapling forks into
a girl racing upstairs
from the yard, to enter
this stanza. Now tears

fill her eyes, a mirror's
tears, as her nape knot is
pulled by her mother's
comb; the mother notices,

saying: "In His countenance
are all the valleys made
shining." Her swift hands
plait the rivulet's braid.

Chalk flowers that scribble
the asphalt's black slate

and the hibiscus-bell
tell her she is late,

as surf in the branches
increases like the shoal
of blue-and-white benches
in the government school,

reciting this language
that, on a blackboard,
blinds her like a page
of glare on the road,

so she ambles towards
an inner silence along
a red track the forest
swallows like a tongue.

III

Noon. Dry cicadas whine
like the rusting pedals
of her mother's machine,
then stop. Lime petals

drift like snipt cloth
in the stitched silence;
like pollen, their growth
means her providence.

Noon hems a lime tree
with irregular shade;
from so much symmetry
her back is tired.

The row of Sphinxes
that my eyes rest on
are hills as fixed as
their stony question:

"Can you call each range
by its right name, aloud,
while our features change
between light and cloud?"

But my memory is small
as the sea's thin sound,
what I vaguely recall
is a line of white sand

and lines in the mahogany
of cured faces and stones
muttering under a stony
river, but the questions

dissolving will unravel
their knots—mountain
springs whose gravel
grows hoarse in rain—

as a woodsman relaxes
to hear the sky split
seconds after the axe's
stroke, the names fit

their echo: Mahaut!
Forestière! And far,
the leaf-hoarse echo
of Mabouya! And, ah!

the hill rises and eats
from my hand, the mongrel
yelping happily, repeats
vowel after vowel,

the boughs bow to me,
the dialects applaud
as the sap of memory
races upward.

IV

West of each stanza
that the sunrise made,
banana fields answer
their light; overhead,

a hawk that wheeled,
my heart in its beak,
to the rim of the world
is bringing it back

to the fading bridge,
to the river that turns
in its bed, to the ridge
where the tree returns

from her lessons, late.
Which shack was hers?
Now she climbs straight
up the steps of this verse,

and sits to a supper
of bread and fry-fish

as trees repeat her
darkening English.

Shack windows flare.
Green fireflies arc,
igniting Forestière,
Orléans, Fond St. Jacques,

and the forest runs
sleeping, its eyes shut,
except for one glance
from a lamplit hut;

now, above the closed text
of small shacks that slid
by the headlights: the apex
of a hill like a pyramid.

In the oven-warm night
embers fly. A shop door
flings a panel of light
on the road and an odour

of saltfish. A dry sand
pile scatters in stars.
Cat-like, Pigeon Island
pins the sea in its claws.

Roseau Valley

(For George Odlum)

A shovelful of blackbirds
shot over the road's shoulder
and memory twittered backwards
past the juddering steamroller

gravelling the asphalt road
this sunrise through Roseau
to the sugar mill that roared
to a stop and the widening echo

of canes, when they used to grow
cane in this sweet valley;
then from the canes in arrow,
blackbirds shot in volley

after volley of acolytes,
making every day Sunday
after the strike. No lights
on in the abandoned factory

now. Trolleys rust on ties.
The crop switched to bananas
instead and a boy's paradise
fell in sheaves of hosannas.

Between narrow gauge lines, grass
thickens. A crossing will wait
in vain for the old iron stanzas
to pass with their fragrant freight.

The factory's bleached galvanize
roof buckles. The sheets grapple
with crowbars of wind that prize
its last nails, but the chapel

at Jacmel, whose prayers gently chain
the joined wrists of workers (shoulders
still bent like the murmurous cane,
whatever the crop), stays as old as

the valley, and the litany
flows to the molasses accents
of local priests, not from Brittany
or Alsace-Lorraine. Incense

continues in the same vein
of charcoal smoke on a hill
connecting Roseau to heaven,
but breath went out of the mill.

How green and sweet I kept it
to my aging soul! It shines
when a muscular wind has swept it
with a shadowy scythe, but my lines

led to what? They provided
no comfort like the French priests'
or the Workers Hymn that divided
heaven from a wage increase,

this language that offered its
love few could read, those croppers
who shared communion's profits
or the Union's, for a few coppers.

What use was my praise of its level
green light to those valley-kind
folk? Over chimney and hovel
a cloud's fist closed and darkened

and gestured to the lightning
of crackling, amplified speeches
that broke into a roar of rain
from the irrigation ditches,

and the shirt-assembling flood
gathered in its full force
round the factory gate, then swirled,
bewildered at its next course.

Every scarecrow that had risen
from a ditch with crucified cry
would alarm the factory siren
or the eye of the belfry,

until, like dishevelled cane
after the crop was burnt,
their charred stalks threshed again
under Church and government,

but one Monday road-wide
they marched, sheaves in the fist,
as police bikes purred beside
them towards Government Office,

and the brown river flowed uphill,
its noise coiled round the Morne,
and it left the old sugar mill
to look after its cane alone.

My hand shared the same unrest as
the workers, but what were its powers
to those ragged harvesters
turning my Book of Hours?

Demons snarl in a flag and
smoke coils from a thurifer,
the breath of the opium dragon
makes a Lenin of Lucifer.

Countries of cereal grain
are swept under the shadow
of a scything flag, so the cane
went with the blackbird's arrow,

and, gone with its harvest, what?
My vision that made it once
"orient and immortal wheat"
or the height of indifference?

But was mine a different realm
really? Mitres or pawns can shift
the shadows of a changing regime
over square fields, but my gift

that cannot pay back this island
enough, that gave no communion
of tongues, whose left hand
never lifted the sheaves in union,

still sweats with the trickling resin
in a hill's hot armpit, as
my choice of a road is rising
from the sea's amphitheatres

to inhale a bracing horizon
above belfry or chimney where
the steamroller's heartbeat dies on
blue, indivisible air.

A Latin Primer

(In Memoriam: H. D. Boxill)

I had nothing against which
to notch the growth of my work
but the horizon, no language
but the shallows in my long walk

home, so I shook all the help
my young right hand could use
from the sand-crusted kelp
of distant literatures.

The frigate bird my phoenix,
I was high on iodine,
one drop from the sun's murex
stained the foam's fabric wine;

ploughing white fields of surf
with a boy's shins, I kept
staggering as the shelf
of sand under me slipped,

then found my deepest wish
in the swaying words of the sea,
and the skeletal fish
of that boy is ribbed in me;

but I saw how the bronze
dusk of imperial palms
curled their fronds into questions
over Latin exams.

I hated signs of scansion.
Those strokes across the line
drizzled on the horizon
and darkened discipline.

They were like Mathematics
that made delight Design,
arranging the thrown sticks
of stars to sine and cosine.

Raging, I'd skip a pebble
across the sea's page; it still
scanned its own syllable:
trochee, anapest, dactyl.

Miles, foot soldier. *Fossa,*
a trench or a grave. My hand
hefts a last sand bomb to toss
at slowly fading sand.

I failed Matriculation
in Maths; passed it; after that,
I taught Love's basic Latin:
Amo, amas, amat.

In tweed jacket and tie
a master at my college
I watched the old words dry
like seaweed on the page.

I'd muse from the roofed harbour
back to my desk, the boys'
heads plunged in paper
softly as porpoises.

The discipline I preached
made me a hypocrite;
their lithe black bodies, beached,
would die in dialect;

I spun the globe's meridian,
showed its sealed hemispheres,
but where were those brows heading
when neither world was theirs?

Silence clogged my ears
with cotton, a cloud's noise;
I climbed white tiered arenas
trying to find my voice,

and I remember: it was on a
Saturday near noon, at Vigie,
that my heart, rounding the corner
of Half-Moon Battery,

stopped to watch the foundry
of midday cast in bronze
the trunk of a gommier tree
on a sea without seasons,

while ochre Rat Island
was nibbling the sea's lace,
that a frigate bird came sailing
through a tree's net, to raise

its emblem in the cirrus,
named with the common sense
of fishermen: sea scissors,
Fregata magnificens,

ciseau-la-mer, the patois
for its cloud-cutting course;
and that native metaphor
made by the strokes of oars,

with one wing beat for scansion,
that slowly levelling V
made one with my horizon
as it sailed steadily

beyond the sheep-nibbled columns
of fallen marble trees,
or the roofless pillars once
sacred to Hercules.

The Villa Restaurant

That terra-cotta waitress,
elbows out, seems to brood
on her own shape, her irises
now slate, now hazel-hued

as pebbles in the shallows
of sunlit river D'Oree;
her ears, curled jars, enclose
small talk and cutlery.

From the red clay of Piaille
this cool carafe was made;
a raw, unfinished people
there ply the potter's trade;

and on his cedar shelf is
jar after jar like this—
maternal at the pelvis
yet girlish at the wrist.

I peel the wet clay slow-
ly of its surrounding cloth,
as the river D'Oree's echo
hums through her parted mouth.

Let statues carved or fired
wear fig leaves for a fly,
or a startled hamadryad
cover her cold thigh.

I have seen their stone eyelids
in marble almonds say:
"Your sea has its own *Iliads*,
Noli me tangere."

So others can look for her
beauty through dusty glass,
in Greek urn or amphora—
I choose the living vase

and turn into a river
whose brown tongue will not rest
until my praises fill the
clay goblets of her breast

with clear-skinned river water
on slate or hazel shale,
from that illiterate quarter
some Frenchman called Choiseul.

But in her is Assam;
the sand towers of Balbec
point when the goblet's arm
massages a stiff neck;

the cracked ground in Mantegna
is hers, the golden apple;
the blue gesso behind her
head is my Sistine Chapel;

striding from the verandah
frame in her cloud-filled bodice,
with the sun behind her
and a freckled forest,

her beauty not her fault as
her palm smooths the flaws
of linen laid like altars
with crumbs and today's flowers.

The Three Musicians

(For Hunter François)

"Once Christmas coming
it have a breeze as
fresh as Bethlehem in
the glorious cedars.

From town to Vieuxfort,
Vieuxfort to Castries,
it does varnish the road
through the villages.

We does put red tins
on the porch for pardon,
we whitewash the stones
from the first garden;

in the sprinkled yard
by the white rose tree
is the soft dent made
by an angel's knee,

whose robes so pure
they does pleat like when
water twists from a ewer
of porcelain;

so for young and old
life refresh. That week,
break a lime leaf, it cold
as an archangel's cheek,

whose shadow, swift
up the hillside grass,
does make cedars lift
so his wings can pass,"

sings Madame Isidor,
her front step scoured
for her first visitor,
Our barefoot Lord.

He was poorer than them,
no place for his bed;
"My parlour is Jerusalem,
my table, Gilead."

Whole week she practise
her bow: "Pleased to meet you;
this one here? That is
Joseph, carpenter too."

And that whole week self,
if one vex, next one laugh;
from the glass case Joseph
sets the silver carafe

by two pillars of gold
Johnnie Walker whisky,
let old people get old,
not Joseph, he brisk, brisk, he

hugging her like his craft,
he stop going to café,
he only singing: "Half
the Herald Angels"; Saturday

he come in a transport from
the market straight home;
a cannon of linoleum
unfurls in their room.

Now the ham there bubbling
for all it's worth
in a kerosene tin
wrapped tight in grey cloth,

and everywhere the earth
smell of raisins, a black cake
she will cut for the birth
of the child she can't make.

Ah, Christmas, Christmas morning!
They hear on the wind,
the whine and warning
of Ti-Boy's violin;

they feel the Blood
of the Innocents pass
through the Roman blade
of poinsettias,

as the three musicians
passing yard after yard,
where the ginger's fragrance
is spikenard;

the cuatro strumming
to their gravelly carol,
they reach. "Come in, come in,
it have whisky, sorrel—"

Sorrel with its bloody crown
of thorns, by the fence
where the lace bush kneels down
in penitence—

"Joseph, bring three chairs!"
They bow at her door.
Three felt hats. One says,
"*Bon Noël*, Ma' Isidor,

I am Frank Incense,
Mr. Gold, Mr. Myrrh."
They rest their instruments
with care in a corner.

New hats on their knees,
they nod at how neat
everything is, a breeze
dries their trickling sweat.

One lifts his shot glass
with curled finger, so,
toasting the Mistress,
'cause all of them know

she dream of white lace
on soft ebony skin,
but is somehow God's grace
she cannot make children;

the lifting curtains
brighten the linoleum,
they bring a child's presence
to her varnished room.

They eat in silence
the black cake that she brings,
next to their instruments,
three stiff-backed kings,

who hand back their plates
with a piece on the side
for manners, belt two straights,
then start singing like shite;

in the fiddler's screels
they hunger and thirst
for the child. Joseph feels
that his heart will burst.

Saint Lucia's First Communion

At dusk, on the edge of the asphalt's worn-out ribbon,
in white cotton frock, cotton stockings, a black child stands.
First her, then a small field of her. Ah, it's First Communion!
They hold pink ribboned missals in their hands,

the stiff plaits pinned with their white satin moths.
The caterpillar's accordion, still pumping out the myth
along twigs of cotton from whose parted mouths
the wafer pods in belief without an "if"!

So, all across Saint Lucia thousands of innocents
were arranged on church steps, facing the sun's lens,
erect as candles between squinting parents,
before darkness came on like their blinded saint's.

But if it were possible to pull up on the verge
of the dimming asphalt, before its headlights lance
their eyes, to house each child in my hands,
to lower the window a crack, and delicately urge

the last moth delicately in, I'd let the dark car
enclose their blizzard, and on some black hill,
their pulsing wings undusted, loose them in thousands to
        stagger
heavenward before it came on: the prejudice, the evil!

Gros-Ilet

From this village, soaked like a grey rag in salt water,
a language came, garnished with conch shells,
with a suspicion of berries in its armpits
and elbows like flexible oars. Every ceremony commenced
in the troughs, in the middens, at the daybreak and the daydark
     funerals
attended by crabs. The odours were fortified
by the sea. The anchor of the islands went deep
but was always clear in the sand. Many a shark,
and often the ray, whose wings are as wide as sails,
rose with insomniac stare from the wavering corals,
and a fisherman held up a catfish like a tendrilled head.
And the night with its certain, inextinguishable candles
was like All Souls' Night upside down, the way a bat keeps
its own view of the world. So their eyes looked down, amused,
on us, and found we were walking strangely,
and wondered about our sense of balance, how we slept
as if we were dead, how we confused
dreams with ordinary things like nails, or roses,
how rocks aged quickly with moss,
the sea made furrows that had nothing to do with time,
and the sand started whirlwinds with nothing to do at all,
and the shadows answered to the sun alone.
And sometimes, like the top of an old tire,
the black rim of a porpoise. Elpenor, you
who broke your arse, drunk, tumbling down the bulkhead,
and the steersman who sails, like the ray under the breathing
     waves,

34

keep moving, there is nothing here for you.
There are different candles and customs here, the dead
are different. Different shells guard their graves.
There are distinctions beyond the paradise
of our horizon. This is not the grape-purple Aegean.
There is no wine here, no cheese, the almonds are green,
the sea grapes bitter, the language is that of slaves.

The Whelk Gatherers

Since hairy nettle, forked mandrake, and malign
toadstool, frog phlegm or bristling spiny urchin,
are, by their nature, poisons, we should not question
what the moon-eyed whelk gatherers mutter they have seen.
Who is this prince? How is he helmeted?
We watch high carrion frigates grow more common,
we see that our breath makes indecisive shapes,
but what disturbs him on the drenched ramparts,
staring at stars like the insomniac sea?
What cloaked rumours run through the kingdom,
hiding from the night watchmen's lanterns in wet streets?
Slapped by our inquisitors, the whelk pickers only gibber:
"He is like a shell soldered to the sea stone,
and there's no knife to prize it."

                      The subtle torturers
pretend to agree. The prelate's modern sermon
proves there is no evil, mere misdirected will,
but the eyes of the whelk gatherers are as grey as oysters
and his black sail slithers slowly under their mossed keel.

"It is Abaddon the usurper on whose heart the toad sticks."
"There is nothing under his helmet but your fear."
"He has drunk the sucked-out shells of his own eyes,
and his sword hilt is gripped by scaly talons."
"And he reappears after you have made the crucifix?"
"Yes. The sea scorpion trots to his whistle like a dog."
"In his acid spittle the vultures unfurl their umbrellas,
and the sea shines like his chain mail through the fog.

He fastens on the neck of this world and will not be prized."
When we give them broth, and this goes on for nights,
the youngest stares in the steam till it gets cold.
"If it is Abaddon the usurper, what will he usurp?"
He shudders. "May seraphs stand against him in silver sheaves."

We explain it is mutinous moonlight on the waves,
it is fishermen's moonshine, that they are merely crazed
from the salt cuts in their palms, yet each one believes
it is Abaddon, that what stands on the drenched seawall,
shuddering ribbed wings like a wet mongrel,
erect as a stingray, is a devilfish, not the devil;
but the youngest repeats in a voice inhuman
from hoarseness like surf wearily withdrawn
from whelk-ulcered rock: "If it is not him, then
why do the black-cloaked clouds claw at the moon
and smother her round scream like a madwoman?"
Eyes wild as whelks over the lifted spoon.

White Magic

(For Leo St. Helene)

The *gens-gagée* kicks off her wrinkled skin.
Clap her soul in a jar! The half-man wolf
can trot with bending elbows, rise, and grin
in lockjawed lycanthropia. Censers dissolve
the ground fog with its whistling, wandering souls,
the unbaptized, unfinished, and uncursed
by holy fiat. The island's griots love
our mushroom elves, the devil's parasols
who creep like grubs from a trunk's rotten holes,
their mouths a sewn seam, their clubfeet reversed.
Exorcism cannot anachronize
those signs we hear past midnight in a wood
where a pale woman like a blind owl flies
to her forked branch, with scarlet moons for eyes
bubbling with doubt. You heard a silver splash?
It's nothing. If it slid from mossed rocks
dismiss it as a tired crab, a fish,
unless our water-mother with dank locks
is sliding under this page below your pen,
only a simple people think they happen.
Dryads and hamadryads were engrained
in the wood's bark, in papyrus, and this paper;
but when our dry leaves crackle to the deer-
footed, hobbling hunter, Papa Bois,
he's just Pan's clone, one more translated satyr.
The crone who steps from her jute sugar sack
(though you line moonlit lintels with white flour),
the *beau l'homme* creeping towards you, front to back,

the ferny footed, faceless, mouse-eared elves,
these fables of the backward and the poor
marbled by moonlight, will grow white and richer.
Our myths are ignorance, theirs are literature.

A Letter from the Old Guard

(For Irene Worth)

From a palm-stirred province in the Antilles,
a veteran dips his quill in sea-blue ink

to commemorate the ferocity of the Gurkhas
and his own regiment lost in the sandy hills

of the Sudan; he hears the chink-a-chink
of brass and cymbals, when the crowd's outcry

kept the pigeons circling Piccadilly Circus—
and they were the pride of Alexander's eye.

Now, in the wake of peace for forty years,
gales lift Hyde Park, a statue like a ship

divides the leaves; it is that noise he hears,
a tongue of surf moistening his upper lip,

and writes:
                "Ladies, I saw you on your balcony
on Brazil Street, the sunset rouged your cheek

"and touched me. Please, I don't want money,
but is Remembrance Day, so, all this week,

"I thought, as, doubtless, you, about the war,
two widowed sisters in the same white collar

"as your lace balcony facing Columbus Square,
there, as a sea scout on Empire Day,

"I saw you, with your hair cut differently,
under cream Leghorn hats; you were both fair

"and bright. Bulwen was Administrator,
a Welshman, but nobody didn't mind.

"All is so clear now I recall to mind
the rustling plumes of the four Royal Palms,

"I hear a silver music when the fountain's
tears splash our cheeks; then by the monument,

"The sergeant-major's shout frighten the mountains,
and as six hundred boots Presented Arms,

"the flag fold from the four points of the Empire,
while Bulwen growl this passage from the Psalms:

" 'I will look to the hills . . .' The hills remain.
Our hair is ashes, but our hearts is fire.

"I never passed under your high verandah
as a boy. Town had its private precincts,

"but I enlist, and I can tell you, I pass under
heavy mortar fire; I have seen the Sphinx,

"with its old boxer's face rest on the sands;
I know that both you ladies lost your husbands

"fighting Rommel, but the small white flowers that come
out of the sand is soldiers' hearts; a sea

"of sand was my black regiment's home,
bless Field Marshal Viscount Montgomery

"and bless them all, the Mall, the brass and crimson
of the Horse Guards; I was twelve years of age

"when Edward abdicate for Mrs. Simpson,
but even today, I can recall my rage!

"I served with Lord Alexander in the Sudan,
I know his batman, I am now a night watchman.

"Then we get Independence all of a sudden,
and something went. We can't run anything,

"we black people. So far, I have not found one
I would trust. I soldiered for my King

"and island. My hands catch arthritis,
but they rendered unto Caesar what is Caesar's,

"just like the Gurkhas. What ferocious blighters!
Still, we was good as them. Now I will cease, as

"from my pen's eye, I see, has dropped a tear.
Forgive the blot as you forgive the writer's

"name. Let this be, ladies, secretly yours . . ."
Then tears the letter up, as sovereign years

ring on a platter from brass-bright Benares
on Vigie Barracks in the exaggerated light

of the Raj, darkening like a teak cabinet
and the palms' night surf and a cold supper set

under a brass-buttoned postcard of the pier
at Brighton when our wars were happier.

Storm Figure

The nineteenth century, like a hurricane lamp,
haloed, last night, the boards of a kitchen table.
With the lamp poles down, its wick smoke pined and flamed,
singeing the mind's ceiling like a Hardy novel.

Barefoot on the cold grass outside the beach house,
you see fresh channels furrowing the beach's dreck,
then a far, smoky figure where brown shallows
roll fallen trunks like bodies from a shipwreck.

The wrong time. The wrong ground. The Wessex coast
is in another century. The lamp's eye of flame
at its barred window, throughout the storm's harvest,
was once Fidelity. She has changed her name.

The shallows' mutterings suit her
thunder-gone waiting, clouds blowing in smoky scraps,
breakers that chuff; long, leaden swells of pewter,
the pier piles grumbling, mosses gripped by crabs.

Drop by slow drop each branch loses its pearls,
surf drags soiled petticoats through the beach's muck,
ice fetters her ankles fording the new rock pools,
sheet spray obscures her, but she is its watermark;

Current returns. Lights dot the wrecked roads.
To the morse of crickets this century takes shape.
The more you walk, the farther she recedes,
a figurehead fluttering without a ship.

Now sunshine with its mullioned mackerel dances
over lamp and novel by the double bed,
rippling the oval where her drowned face glances
till the circle of one century has settled.

On drying scarps, with loops of tidal grass,
her shadow fades into the clouding sand;
surf lifts its hem to let a low seagull pass
arrowing in silence, which is the soul's sound.

Marina Tsvetaeva

Newspapers aged in an armchair, the sofa drowsed
in sunlit vacancy. In the beach house one bed
kept its plaid coverlet smooth; the mirror was crossed
and recrossed by a ceiling fan's shadowy blade.

Parched as the beach, I stepped into the kitchen.
My thirst growled in the rusty faucet.
A gust from the open fridge showed that white lichen
had crusted the ice trays to a Siberian forest.

I drank from the frosted bottle in my self-allowed
happiness. The ceiling blades rattled in peace.
I saw that the unhinged door of a varnished cupboard
leaned like a violin's cheekbone cradled on space.

I put the iced water back and saw a station's
stalled train welded in ice. Round a windowsill,
frost crocheted your face; in drops of patience,
a gull's cry melted like an icicle.

You slip from the door of your book in a black cloak—
its characters run in the rain, like the old mascara
of the Wailing Wall, like the porcelain crack
in a doll's grin—your lashes streaked with kohl.

Through the fly screen, a leaf of lime or laurel
has learnt your silence. The other tongue. Does
the vine's wrist pulse, every green tendril
curl from your throat? Houseflies couple and buzz

on the single bed, but, ah, your laddering lark's
interrupted song! The seaweed's Cyrillics
are your life's shorthand, the sandpiper's footmarks
your dashes and hyphens, the sand's broken sticks.

It's hurricane season, Tsvetaeva; some days it rains
and the sea stands head downward like a horse
or a girl over a basin, and then the choked drains
give rein to all their sorrows with full force,

but out of the blue, sometimes a seagull cries
like thorns on bleached driftwood. The Godhead grows
further and bluer; then, beyond dunes of prose,
runs the exclamation mark of your small figure.

And the seaweed dries out her hair, Marina Tsvetaeva,
the pelican breaks its flight like a crucifix;
but that bridal, circling survivor
the seagull, in her grace affects

this beach house, a dresser, a sky-blue powder box,
the horizon's hyphen, the blank wall—a passport
from which they peeled your photograph, a bed clock's
pointless ticking, a yellow butterfly dress that you forgot,

sand brushed from my bedsheet, the grave of a pillow,
an oceanic tear. The sun swings its scales.
Time, that's half of eternity, like the sea in a window,
billows your pages' stationary sails.

The Light of the World

Kaya now, got to have kaya now,
Got to have kaya now,
For the rain is falling.
—BOB MARLEY

Marley was rocking on the transport's stereo
and the beauty was humming the choruses quietly.
I could see where the lights on the planes of her cheek
streaked and defined them; if this were a portrait
you'd leave the highlights for last, these lights
silkened her black skin; I'd have put in an earring,
something simple, in good gold, for contrast, but she
wore no jewelry. I imagined a powerful and sweet
odour coming from her, as from a still panther,
and the head was nothing else but heraldic.
When she looked at me, then away from me politely
because any staring at strangers is impolite,
it was like a statue, like a black Delacroix's
Liberty Leading the People, the gently bulging
whites of her eyes, the carved ebony mouth,
the heft of the torso solid, and a woman's,
but gradually even that was going in the dusk,
except the line of her profile, and the highlit cheek,
and I thought, O Beauty, you are the light of the world!

It was not the only time I would think of that phrase
in the sixteen-seater transport that hummed between
Gros-Islet and the Market, with its grit of charcoal
and the litter of vegetables after Saturday's sales,
and the roaring rum shops, outside whose bright doors
you saw drunk women on pavements, the saddest of all things,
winding up their week, winding down their week.

The Market, as it closed on this Saturday night,
remembered a childhood of wandering gas lanterns
hung on poles at street corners, and the old roar
of vendors and traffic, when the lamplighter climbed,
hooked the lantern on its pole and moved on to another,
and the children turned their faces to its moth, their
eyes white as their nighties; the Market
itself was closed in its involved darkness
and the shadows quarrelled for bread in the shops,
or quarrelled for the formal custom of quarrelling
in the electric rum shops. I remember the shadows.

The van was slowly filling in the darkening depot.
I sat in the front seat, I had no need for time.
I looked at two girls, one in a yellow bodice
and yellow shorts, with a flower in her hair,
and lusted in peace, the other less interesting.
That evening I had walked the streets of the town
where I was born and grew up, thinking of my mother
with her white hair tinted by the dyeing dusk,
and the tilting box houses that seemed perverse
in their cramp; I had peered into parlours
with half-closed jalousies, at the dim furniture,
Morris chairs, a centre table with wax flowers,
and the lithograph of *Christ of the Sacred Heart*,
vendors still selling to the empty streets—
sweets, nuts, sodden chocolates, nut cakes, mints.

An old woman with a straw hat over her headkerchief
hobbled towards us with a basket; somewhere,
some distance off, was a heavier basket
that she couldn't carry. She was in a panic.
She said to the driver: *"Pas quittez moi à terre,"*
which is, in her patois: "Don't leave me stranded,"
which is, in her history and that of her people:

"Don't leave me on earth," or, by a shift of stress:
"Don't leave me the earth" [for an inheritance];
"*Pas quittez moi à terre*, Heavenly transport,
Don't leave me on earth, I've had enough of it."
The bus filled in the dark with heavy shadows
that would not be left on earth; no, that would be left
on the earth, and would have to make out.
Abandonment was something they had grown used to.

And I had abandoned them, I knew that there
sitting in the transport, in the sea-quiet dusk,
with men hunched in canoes, and the orange lights
from the Vigie headland, black boats on the water;
I, who could never solidify my shadow
to be one of their shadows, had left them their earth,
their white rum quarrels, and their coal bags,
their hatred of corporals, of all authority.
I was deeply in love with the woman by the window.
I wanted to be going home with her this evening.
I wanted her to have the key to our small house
by the beach at Gros-Ilet; I wanted her to change
into a smooth white nightie that would pour like water
over the black rocks of her breasts, to lie
simply beside her by the ring of a brass lamp
with a kerosene wick, and tell her in silence
that her hair was like a hill forest at night,
that a trickle of rivers was in her armpits,
that I would buy her Benin if she wanted it,
and never leave her on earth. But the others, too.

Because I felt a great love that could bring me to tears,
and a pity that prickled my eyes like a nettle,
I was afraid I might suddenly start sobbing
on the public transport with the Marley going,
and a small boy peering over the shoulders

of the driver and me at the lights coming,
at the rush of the road in the country darkness,
with lamps in the houses on the small hills,
and thickets of stars; I had abandoned them,
I had left them on earth, I left them to sing
Marley's songs of a sadness as real as the smell
of rain on dry earth, or the smell of damp sand,
and the bus felt warm with their neighbourliness,
their consideration, and the polite partings

in the light of its headlamps. In the blare,
in the thud-sobbing music, the claiming scent
that came from their bodies. I wanted the transport
to continue forever, for no one to descend
and say a good night in the beams of the lamps
and take the crooked path up to the lit door,
guided by fireflies; I wanted her beauty
to come into the warmth of considerate wood,
to the relieved rattling of enamel plates
in the kitchen, and the tree in the yard,
but I came to my stop. Outside the Halcyon Hotel.
The lounge would be full of transients like myself.
Then I would walk with the surf up the beach.
I got off the van without saying good night.
Good night would be full of inexpressible love.
They went on in their transport, they left me on earth.

Then, a few yards ahead, the van stopped. A man
shouted my name from the transport window.
I walked up towards him. He held out something.
A pack of cigarettes had dropped from my pocket.
He gave it to me. I turned, hiding my tears.
There was nothing they wanted, nothing I could give them
but this thing I have called "The Light of the World."

Oceano Nox

(For Robert Lee)

What sort of moon will float up through the almonds
like a bobbing marker in the surf of trees?
A quarter-moon, like an Iranian dagger?
A capitol with wide spheres of influence?
One with a birthmark like Gorbachev's head?
A local moon, full of its own importance,
a watchman's flashlight with fresh batteries,
startling the trickle from a kitchen drain,
pinning a crab to the hotel's wire fence,
changing its mind like a cat burglar,
probing locked harbours, rattling the foam's chain.

Calm as a kitchen clock without the hands
high on a cupboard shelf of this beach house,
the moon stares on a plastic tablecloth,
where she reprints the shadow of a mouse
bent like a friar nibbling his rosary's
berries with fingers quicker than his mouth;
then islands were the gems of an Infanta,
and tiny armoured ants, in Indian file,
hoisted their banners, singing "Sancta, Sancta
Regina," then scattered in armadas
to the cracked wedding cake of her fixed smile.

Her forehead bound as tightly as a nun's
or a black laundress who has pinned the sails,
forgotten, on a clothesline, she was once
the Virgin Queen whose radiance drew the snails

of her horned galleons with their silvery slime,
pale slugs in sand. Insomniac remorse.
Beyond all that now, and way past her prime
her mind is wandering in another tense;
she hears the cannon's surf, the palm frond's gales,
and sees, through the erasures of her face,
those wrecks she christened: *Invincible, Revenge.*

Oceano Nox. Night whispers to the Ocean.
A watchman in a constable's cloak patrols
the hotel's wire boundary. I answer his good night.
His flashlight swivels through a spume of salt,
it passes over the old hill of skulls
made by husked coconut shells, the original fault
unsettled by the shallows' dark commotion;
he sings a reggae in a moon so bright
you can read palms by it. A steel band rolls
glissandos of surf round the hotel pool's
gazebo, doubling the moon's arc light.

A wave of sound, an echo overhead
(not shaking the moon's oval in the pool),
that pulses in the memory, when, from school
to college, I cherished the theatre
of high Marlovian clouds, my heritage
of that great globe herself, and what I read
sank in like surf reopening the wet
pores of sand, and swirls in the cave's head,
till on this beach-house wall, centuries later,
I mutter the sea's lines, and they recede
to the emerald and ruby of a fading jet:

"Black is the beauty of the brightest day,"
black the circumference around her rings

that radiate from black invisibly,
black is the music which her round mouth sings,
black is the backcloth on which diadems shine,
black, night's perfection, which conceals its flaws
except the crack of the horizon's line;
now all is changing but my focus was
once on the full moon, not what surrounds the moon,
upon a watchman's flashlight not the watchman,
the mesmerizing wake of History.

I have rehearsed their beauty all this week,
and her white disk moves like a camera's lens
along the ebony of a high-boned cheek,
I mean Anne Daniels's, Lauretta Etienne's,
their bow-carved mouths, their half-globed eyes serene,
surfaces so polished that their skin would squeak
if you pushed your forefinger up the bone,
their laughter white as breakers in their grin,
too modest to be actresses, each one
wrapped in sea cotton, intact from Benin.

Oceano Nox. The clocks resume their motion,
a laser from the lighthouse skims a wave;
a different age is whispering to the ocean,
the fronds will take the old moon by the hand
and lead her gently into a cloud's grave;
I cross the darkened grass back to the house;
then all her radiance comes back again,
making the frogs sundials on the lawn;
there is a ring around her, meaning rain,
and meaning nothing more, in that blank face,
than History's innocence or its remorse.

So let her light dissolve into the sable
and velvet memory of a collared cloud,

dimming the square tiles on a kitchen table,
dulling the cheers of an applauding crowd
of breakers flinging whitecaps into space
when you close in the door and ram the latch, as
you think of women with their necks as supple
as bowing palms, and watch the mouse scuttle
back to its hole. A palm's nib scratches
the roof's parchment. At a brass lamp's base,
new rainflies, and the masts of wooden matches.

A scribbling plague of rainflies. Go to bed.
After the morning rain, the shuddering almond
will shake the sweat of nightmare from its bent head.
The surf will smooth the sand's page and even
the cumuli change their idea of heaven
as the sun wipes the nib of a palm frond,
and from the wet hills, parishes of birds
test a new tongue, because these are their shores,
while the old moon gapes at a loss for words
like any ghost at cockcrow, as a force
threshes the palms, lifting their hearts and yours.

Night Fishing

Line, trawl for each word
with the home-sick toss
of a black pirogue anchored
in stuttering phosphorus.

The crab-fishers' torches
keep to the surf's crooked line,
and a cloud's page scorches
with a smell of kerosene.

Thorny stars halo
the sybil's black cry:
"*Apothenein thelo*
I am longing to die."

But, line, live in the sounds
that ignorant shallows use;
then throw the silvery nouns
to open-mouthed canoes.

To Norline

This beach will remain empty
for more slate-coloured dawns
of lines the surf continually
erases with its sponge,

and someone else will come
from the still-sleeping house,
a coffee mug warming his palm
as my body once cupped yours,

to memorize this passage
of a salt-sipping tern,
like when some line on a page
is loved, and it's hard to turn.

E L S E W H E R E

Eulogy to W. H. Auden

(Read at the Cathedral of St. John the Divine,
New York, October 17, 1983)

I

Assuredly, that fissured face
is wincing deeply, and must loathe
our solemn rubbish,
frown on our canonizing farce
as self-enhancing, in lines both
devout and snobbish.

Yet it may spare us who convene
against its wish in varnished pews
this autumn evening;
as maps remember countries, mien
defines a man, and his appears
at our beseeching.

Each granite feature, cracked and plain
as the ground in Giotto, is
apt to this chancel,
the wry mouth bracketed with pain,
the lizard eyes whose motto is:
Opposites cancel.

For further voices will delight
in all that left the body of
the mortal Auden
centuries after candlelit
Kirchstetten freed its tenant of
Time and its burden;

for what we cherish is as much
our own fate, stricken with the light
of his strange calling,
and, once we leave this darkened church
and stand on pavements in the night
to see a falling

leaf like a seraph sign the arc
made by a street lamp, and move on
to selfish futures,
our footsteps echoing in the dark
street have, for their companion,
his shadow with us.

Autumn is when small wars begin
drunken offensives; the skies spin
with reeling scanners;
but you, who left each feast at nine,
knew war, like free verse, is a sign
of awful manners.

Tonight, as every dish deploys
from sonar peaks its amplified
fireside oration,
we keep yours to ourselves, a voice
internal, intricately wired
as our salvation.

11

In your flat world of silence
the fissures made by speech

close. A sandpiper signs
the margin of a beach.

Soon, from the whistling tundras,
geese following earth's arc
will find an accurate Indies
in the lime-scented dark.

Our conjugations, Master,
are still based on the beat
of wings that gave their cast to
our cuneiform alphabet,

though shredders hum with rage through
the neon afternoon,
and dials guide earth's marriage
to an irascible moon;

not needling Arcturus,
nor Saturn's visible hum
have, on their disks, a chorus
of epithalamium;

the farther the space station
from the Newtonian shelf,
the more man's conversation,
increases with himself.

Once, past a wooden vestry,
down still colonial streets,
the hoisted chords of Wesley
were strong as miners' throats;

in treachery and in union,
despite your Empire's wrong,

I made my first communion
there, with the English tongue.

It was such dispossession
that made possession joy,
when, strict as Psalm or Lesson,
I learnt your poetry.

III

Twilight. Grey pigeons batten
on St. Mark's slate. A face
startles us with its pattern
of sunlit fire escapes.

Your slippered shadow pities
the railings where it moves,
brightening with *Nunc Dimittis*
the city it still loves.

O craft, that strangely chooses
one mouth to speak for all,
O Light no dark refuses,
O Space impenetrable,

fix, among constellations,
the spark we honour here,
whose planetary patience
repeats his earthly prayer

that the City may be Just,
and humankind be kind.
A barge moves, caked with rust
in the East River wind,

and the mouths of all the rivers
are still, and the estuaries
shine with the wake that gives the
craftsman the gift of peace.

Elsewhere

(*For Stephen Spender*)

Somewhere a white horse gallops with its mane
plunging round a field whose sticks
are ringed with barbed wire, and men
break stones or bind straw into ricks.

Somewhere women tire of the shawled sea's
weeping, for the fishermen's dories
still go out. It is blue as peace.
Somewhere they're tired of torture stories.

That somewhere there was an arrest.
Somewhere there was a small harvest
of bodies in the truck. Soldiers rest
somewhere by a road, or smoke in a forest.

Somewhere there is the conference rage
at an outrage. Somewhere a page
is torn out, and somehow the foliage
no longer looks like leaves but camouflage.

Somewhere there is a comrade,
a writer lying with his eyes wide open
on mattress ticking, who will not read
this, or write. How to make a pen?

And here we are free for a while, but
elsewhere, in one-third, or one-seventh
of this planet, a summary rifle butt
breaks a skull into the idea of a heaven

where nothing is free, where blue air
is paper-frail, and whatever we write
will be stamped twice, a blue letter,
its throat slit by the paper knife of the state.

Through these black bars
hollowed faces stare. Fingers
grip the cross bars of these stanzas
and it is here, because somewhere else

their stares fog into oblivion
thinly, like the faceless numbers
that bewilder you in your telephone
diary. Like last year's massacres.

The world is blameless. The darker crime
is to make a career of conscience,
to feel through our own nerves the silent scream
of winter branches, wonders read as signs.

Steam

(For *Leslie Epstein*)

Shawled women shoosh black rooks from a stubble field.
They rise like letters, they resettle in swastikas.
A red star shines on a sickle, the same women fold
a seven-branched candlestick into a mattress.

In a copper twilight some Judith peels an onion
almost to the heart. Brass bases drone their belief.
Gloved fists pound the kitchen door. She eases it open.
The head of Holofernes rots on a paring knife.

I remember bird-boned Grandma chirruping to the squeak
of a piled axle. One note high, one low.
Bicycles, barrows, prams, wagons as long as a week
in the fog at the field's edge, a stream that will flow

to the end of this earth. Star-muzzled moles
would smell us coming and quietly withdraw,
gloving their velvet hides back into holes.
The stars themselves did nothing, but they saw.

When your own name sounds odd, you're in
a foreign province. They shouted ours in columns
on somewhere Strasse under the black rook's reign.
The drizzle counted our skulls. We became sums.

I believe in 10. In my hands. But more than 1,000,000
tires them like crabs. All those bald zeros
add up to a lie, to the eggs of lice milling
in a child's haircut with its shaven furrows.

But Art was with us. Our shirts were the bars
of manuscripts fed into ovens.
Through the smudged sockets of eyes hollow as oboes
we heard those trembling scherzos of Beethoven's,

then huddled, Adam-shy. In a tiled corner
a flue hissed. Father, if we felt betrayed,
forgive our ghosts who thought the Zyklon's sauna
erased You, in whose image we were made.

Like trees in fog, men are still ambling forks
crossing a furrowed field around whose rim
smoke rises from a midden or a gasworks
clouding this globe, making the crystal dim.

A window cracked can thin the temperature
of a steaming bath, a mirror's wisping hair;
the zeros bubbling in bald, cobbled water
with the plug pulled will gurgle and disappear,

but the fog from potato fields, the error
John Webster called "a general mist," condensed
in the stubborn clouding of a bathroom mirror,
cannot be cleaned by faster circling hands.

Central America

Helicopters are cutlassing the wild bananas.
Between a nicotine thumb and forefinger
brittle faces crumble like tobacco leaves.
Children waddle in vests, their legs bowed,
little shrimps curled under their navels.
The old men's teeth are stumps in a charred forest.
Their skins grate like the iguana's.
Their gaze like slate stones.
Women squat by the river's consolations
where children wade up to their knees,
and a stick stirs up a twinkling of butterflies.
Up there, in the blue acres
of forest, flies circle their fathers.
In spring, in the upper provinces
of the Empire, yellow tanagers
float up through the bare branches.
There is no distinction in these distances.

Roman Peace

Declining fast as the leaves in Germania's forest,
senile Augustus would shout for his hacked legions
down erect colonnades. The old man grew more depressed
at this one defeat than from his victories. Well, living legends
constrict in mania and morbidity.
Manacled torches magnify his shadow
going to bed, and his sandals scrape
like a stick raking through rotten, leathery leaves.
He forces withered branches through the sleeves
of his cotton nightgown, and prays for rest.
The single lance of a candle will guard his sleep.
The marble phlegm of Rome lies on his chest.
The Sphinx stares on the sand with lidless eyes.
My legion, my legion, let the old man weep—
the grave is shallower than young Alexander's sighs.

The foraging, the chipped swords, the fire-bright iron
rest like tongues in their scabbards. A bat
circles the milky courtyard, a coin
with an eaten profile races the stars
toward Germany, where the legion's lances have all
grown leaves since the infamous war, and wounds of combat
are stitched with moss. An owl stares
and drinks the moonlight with its saucer eyes.
Just an owl. Not Minerva. The throne,
with no arse to warm it, lengthens its shadow. A rat
with a quivering nose raises a question,
then, doubting such peace, scuttles like a leaf down the wall.

Salsa

The Morro has one eye, a slit.
It is hard grey stone, it is visored
like a scraped conquistador's helmet.
These days not much happens around it.
The palm frond rusts like a Castilian sword.

But there, the women have pomegranate skins
and eyes like black olives, and hair that shines
blue as a crow's wing, if they are Indians.
And the Indians there were Toltec and I forget
what else. But at the Ramada and Holiday Inns,
in water-plumed lounges with wet
plants, a salsa combo sings:

> "Ay, *caramba, gringo!*
> *Is getting like New York!*
> *or Miami, mi amigo, the lingo*
> *the hustling palm trees talk.*"

By the rusty and white walls of Cartagena,
a tree reads the palm of the sand,
but the lines fade quickly; "Malagueña"
grates from a sun-straw-hatted band,
and a cockerel comes striding with its Quetzalcoatl
plumes, and the blackened palm fronds are cattle
barbecued by brigands, just like the Hilton's.
Every dusk there is the death rattle
of the shoal like maracas,
and a wind like a bamboo whistle,
xylophones of bones in the grass.

Sunday in the Old Republic

Where a cathedral shows
its sun-sliced orange face,
arches fanned and roseate,
and a black-tasselled carriage

clops from past centuries
through the black iron gates
of the park that breathes
through those ribs, maids

curse their stumbling kids
near the artificial lakes
floating with strolling crowds
of lilies, a bearded *fin-de-siècle*

rests its arm on the moustache curl
of an iron bench. Silk hats,
clouds' crumpled linen coats,
and dragonflies whose gauze

wings fade like rainbows.
Lies. It was never like this.
There never was any peace
in the spokes of parasols,

for peace only exists
in the leaf-shadowed prose
of the imaginary republic, its
Impressionist canvases.

Down the path, the old peach-
coloured path, a vet's
barrel organ goes, a patch
for one eye, to his marmoset's

questioning tail and eyes
that seem always amazed
at the chain around its waist
and at the nurses' cries

at the children on the edge
of the darkening pasture,
where a swan and her cygnets
sail faster and faster

down the cold current.

French Colonial. "Vers de Société"

I cannot look a veteran in the eye,
or an ambassador, or finish the prose
of autobiographies, blocks of history,
or stroll down boulevards long as operas.

Maurois, or Mauriac—but not Malraux,
the morose Marxist, prophet of *Man's Fate*—
in something I read many years ago
that stuck, without an accurate memory of the date,

compared the symmetry of a work of art
to an hourglass. The French are very good at these
sort of thing; every other frog is a Descartes:
Cogito ergo, that precise *bêtise*.

I memorize the atmosphere in Martinique
as comfortable colonial—tobacco, awnings, Peugeots, pink
    gendarmes,
their pride in a language that I dared not speak
as casually as the gesticulating palms

before Algeria and Dien Bien Phu—
their nauseous sense of heritage and order
revolving around Josephine's or Schoelcher's statue,
and that it was a culture that abhorred water,

and tainted everything with the right taste—
the light, the punches, the Cinzano on the ashtrays.

Our town was named after the Marquis de Castres,
like the general who lost France to the Vietnamese.

That is not important. Now the only thing as great
as an empire is a diva. An hourglass. It's why
the most symmetrical digit is an 8—
spectacles aside, a round-winged Butterfly.

Mimi, the Near-Suicide

Somebody told her she had sad, interesting eyes.
After that, that was it. She stopped by the bridge.
She studied the river's coiled, interesting dyes.
Must drop in for a visit. Good career move:
Ophelia, Mrs. Woolf, and that *feministe garbage*.
A much better ending than plain, provincial love:
a sodden sidewalk, a soaked brown paper bag.

Fame

This is Fame: Sundays,
an emptiness
as in Balthus,

cobbled alleys,
sunlit, aureate,
a wall, a brown tower

at the end of a street,
a blue without bells,
like a dead canvas

set in its white
frame, and flowers:
gladioli, lame

gladioli, stone petals
in a vase. The choir's
sky-high praise

turned off. A book
of prints that turns
by itself. The ticktock

of high heels on a sidewalk.
A crawling clock.
A craving for work.

Tomorrow, Tomorrow

I remember the cities I have never seen
exactly. Silver-veined Venice, Leningrad
with its toffee-twisted minarets. Paris. Soon
the Impressionists will be making sunshine out of shade.
Oh! and the uncoiling cobra alleys of Hyderabad.

To have loved one horizon is insularity;
it blindfolds vision, it narrows experience.
The spirit is willing, but the mind is dirty.
The flesh wastes itself under crumb-sprinkled linens,
widening the *Weltanschauung* with magazines.

A world's outside the door, but how upsetting
to stand by your bags on a cold step as dawn
roses the brickwork and before you start regretting,
your taxi's coming with one beep of its horn,
sidling to the curb like a hearse—so you get in.

Streams

Whenever the sunlit rain
has trawled its trickling meshes
on the dark hills back of the brain,
I keep hearing a Wales
so windswept it refreshes.
Pastures brighten with news
from drizzle-prodded sheep,
and Wales, all its green length,
from wet slate to castle keep,
and the slag hills' runnelling noise
climbs with my mother's voice
in her widowed, timbered strength,
as the pubs turn into pews
and the ale-tongued firelight dies
in talking of Taliesin.

Streams flashed there like buckles,
rooted handshakes of wrists
with corduroy voices would close
on mine, and I heard a language
built of wet stones and mists
in each stubborn bilingual sign,
in the cloud-lit country of Vaughan;
I heard under slag hills the rage
of coal-black abolitionists,
while in the tattered dress
of a lace-torn stream in the sun
the heather-haired princess

bowed with her milk-white stallion
into the embroidered leaves in
the language of Taliesin.

But I saw Wales's capital sin,
I saw Rhondda afflicted with
mineral silence, and a seine
trawl empty Aberystwyth.
Between stricken chimney stacks
on smokeless Sabbaths, starlings
drifted in cinders, curraghs
slept face down on sand, no hymn
rose from the dark throats of the mines
and if, above them, was a lark's
song, it was the only engine
with power 'To Be a Pilgrim'
over paradisal miles in
the country of Taliesin.

I recognized the colonial condition.
In the green coaling station
of our harbour, there were mornes
of anthracite coal, while we prayed
in hard pews, and heard sermons
as empty as wharves, and saw the frayed
knots of miners with minstrel faces
on the wet cobbles, with their patient
caps bared at the evening Mission;
if song is the first submission,
I was humming inside the phrases
of my childhood's faith as I went
in the wake of the rain-lit sun
to the lambs and wet hills of Wales in
the harp-grass of Taliesin.

Winter Lamps

Are they earlier, these
days without afternoons,
whose lamps like crosiers
ask the same questions?

"Will you laugh on the stair
at my fumbling key?
Will your bedroom mirror
stay all day empty?"

Thunderous traffic
shakes snow from a bridge.
Ice floes crack
from the flaw in marriage.

Wind taps my shoulder
to cross on my sign;
crouched engines shudder
at their starting line.

On the sidewalk's sludge
to our lightless house,
I pass the closed church
and its business hours,

along the burnt aisles
of skeletal trees
with no sign of a cardinal's
fiery surplice;

bursitic fingers
on a white fence contract
and the huge iris goes
grey with cataract,

while before me my wish
runs ahead to each room,
turning switch after switch
on to its own welcome;

one of mufflered shadows
on our street, I walk
past orange windows
where marriages work,

raking a moustache
with a tongue that tastes
not your lips, but ash,
in a cold fireplace,

that sour grey ash
such as birch logs make,
spiking every eyelash
in its neuralgic mask,

as the spreading lichen
multiplies its white cells,
our white block as stricken
as that hospital's,

where our child was lost,
as I watched through glass
the white-sheeted ghosts
of the mothers pass.

Snow climbs higher on
the railings, its drifts
shorten the black iron
spikes into arrowheads;

on Brookline's white prairie,
bent, shaggy forms blow—
heads down, thinning out yearly
like the buffalo

in this second Ice Age
that is promised us
by hot gospellers' rage
or white-smocked scientists,

and, at the last lamp,
before the dun door,
I feel winter's cramp
tighter than before.

Spidery damask
laces the panes; it freezes
until the arching mask
of Tragedy sneezes

on theatre façades in our
comic opera, and plaster
flakes fall on the furniture
of shrouded Boston, and faster

than a mine shaft caving in
I can see the black hole
we have made of heaven.
I scrape each boot sole

on the step. Then stamp
at the ice-welded door.
I cannot break through its clamp
to the fire at earth's core.

I am growing more scared of
your queue of dresses
hanging like questions, the love
of a hairpin pierces

me. The key cannot fit.
Either it has swollen
or the brass shrunk. I fight
the lock. Then I lean,

gasping smoke. Despair
can be wide, it can whiten
the Arctic, but it's clear
as I force the door open

that it's not really the end of
this world, but our own,
that I have had enough
of any love with you gone.

The cold light in the oven
grins again at the news.
I tuck our quilt even.
I lie down in my shoes.

By the bed, brown silt
streaks my old coffee cup.
I forgot to buy salt.
I eat standing up.

My faith lost in answers,
apples, firelight, bread,
in windows whose branches
left you cold, and bored.

For Adrian

APRIL 14, 1986

*(To Grace, Ben, Judy, Junior, Norline,
Katryn, Gem, Stanley, and Diana)*

Look, and you will see that the furniture is fading,
that a wardrobe is as insubstantial as a sunset,

that I can see through you, the tissue of your leaves,
the light behind your veins; why do you keep sobbing?

The days run through the light's fingers like dust
or a child's in a sandpit. When you see the stars

do you burst into tears? When you look at the sea
isn't your heart full? Do you think your shadow

can be as long as the desert? I am a child, listen,
I did not invite or invent angels. It is easy

to be an angel, to speak now beyond my eight years,
to have more vestal authority, and to know,

because I have now entered a wisdom, not a silence.
Why do you miss me? I am not missing you, sisters,

neither Judith, whose hair will banner like the leopard's
in the pride of her young bearing, nor Katryn, not Gem

sitting in a corner of her pain, nor my aunt, the one
with the soft eyes that have soothed the one who writes this,

I would not break your heart, and you should know it;
I would not make you suffer, and you should know it;

and I am not suffering, but it is hard to know it.
I am wiser, I share the secret that is only a silence,

with the tyrants of the earth, with the man who piles rags
in a creaking cart, and goes around a corner

of a square at dusk. You measure my age wrongly,
I am not young now, nor old, not a child, nor a bud

snipped before it flowered, I am part of the muscle
of a galloping lion, or a bird keeping low over

dark canes; and what, in your sorrow, in our faces
howling like statues, you call a goodbye

is—I wish you would listen to me—a different welcome,
which you will share with me, and see that it is true.

All this the child spoke inside me, so I wrote it down.
As if his closing grave were the smile of the earth.

Safe Conduct

Rilke was whirled into heaven.
After that, Pasternak.
One smokes with the seraphim,
the other has come back

to plod past frozen ponds
with their harp-wide willows,
his grey forelock a stallion's,
his heart like Akhmatova's,

like a grey horse in winter
that, through thick whirling snow,
as this white page goes whiter,
whinnies, and is here.

Pentecost

Better a jungle in the head
than rootless concrete.
Better to stand bewildered
by the fireflies' crooked street;

winter lamps do not show
where the sidewalk is lost,
nor can these tongues of snow
speak for the Holy Ghost;

the self-increasing silence
of words dropped from a roof
points along iron railings,
direction, if not proof.

But best is this night surf
with slow scriptures of sand,
that sends, not quite a seraph,
but a late cormorant,

whose fading cry propels
through phosphorescent shoal
what, in my childhood gospels,
used to be called the Soul.

The Young Wife

(For Nigel)

Make all your sorrow neat.
Plump pillows, soothe the corners
of her favourite coverlet.
Write to her mourners.

At dusk, after the office,
travel an armchair's ridge,
the valley of the shadow in the sofas,
the drapes' dead foliage.

Ah, but the mirror—the mirror
which you believe has seen
the traitor you feel you are—
clouds, though you wipe it clean!

The buds on the wallpaper
do not shake at the muffled sobbing
the children must not hear,
or the drawers you dare not open.

She has gone with that visitor
that sat beside her, like wind
clicking shut the bedroom door;
arm in arm they went,

leaving her wedding photograph in
its lace frame, a face smiling at
itself. And the telephone
without a voice. The weight

we bear on this heavier side
of the grave brings no comfort.
But the vow that was said
in white lace has brought

you now to the very edge
of that promise; now, for some,
the hooks in the hawthorn hedge
break happily into blossom

and the heart into grief.
The sun slants on a kitchen floor.
You keep setting a fork and knife
at her place for supper.

The children close in the space
made by a chair removed,
and nothing takes her place,
loved and now deeper loved.

The children accept your answer.
They startle you when they laugh.
She sits there smiling that cancer
kills everything but Love.

Summer Elegies

Cynthia, the things we did,
our hands growing more bold as
the unhooked halter slithered
from sunburnt shoulders!

Tremblingly I unfixed it
and two white quarter-moons
unpeeled there like a frisket,
and burnt for afternoons.

We made one shape in water
while in sea grapes a dove
gurgled astonished "Ooos" at
the changing shapes of love.

Time lent us the whole island,
now heat and image fade
like foam lace, like the tan
on a striped shoulder blade.

Salt dried in every fissure,
and, from each sun-struck day,
I peeled the papery tissue
of my dead flesh away;

it feathered as I blew it
from reanointed skin,
feeling love could renew it-
self, and a new life begin.

A halcyon day. No sail.
The sea like cigarette paper
smoothed by a red thumbnail,
then creased to a small square.

The bay shines like tinfoil,
crimps like excelsior;
All the beach chairs are full,
but the beach is emptier.

The snake hangs its old question
on almond or apple tree;
I had her breast to rest on,
the rest was History.

Nothing hurts as much as the word "California,"
the wincing light of Los Angeles. In unfinished Venice
a fresco interrupted in its prophecy looks phonier
than what it promised: gondolas, palazzos, its own Bridge of
    Sighs.
It fades under its graffiti, a transferred paradise.

Sharper than the smell of eucalyptus is the ammonia
of the beach's comfort stations, mist sprayed the air.
My heart could contain the Pacific then, now it is only a-
nother grey waste, with soiled breakers in the flare
of a summer sunset, radios and barbecues. So, here

too the carousel revolves its rusty horizon, lonelier
than an abandoned carnival where the carved white horses
creak to a stop, and the freaks move their paraphernalia
to another beach: Malibu, San Francisco, Santa Barbara.

We recited the names of the avenues, La Cienega,
Pico; I understood the false fronts, the fake Spanish façades,
the dusty brooms of the palms; I was eager
to make a clean sweep, to find the poetry in roof-wide ads

for the latest release, the billboards plugging a Sony, a
new way to live, ours, we were sure, a second-best bet, a Hertz
or an Avis; now so many songs have California
in them, and the H in Hollywood hurts.

I hadn't thought to make light of this: the light of
Los Angeles. I meant it painting the hillside pines.
I meant it, lying under the cool sheets, but it was only the
    right of
any ruin to burst into flowers briefly, strange flowers, fresh
    vines.

There's sometimes more pain in a pop song than all of
    Cambodia,
and that's the trouble, the heart puts love above it
all, any other pain—Chernobyl, a mass murder—
the world's slow stain is there; we cannot remove it.

The irony of it, Cynthia, is that we can never own a-
nother heart. I must smile, or die, hence this lightness.
Hence this fake chic, these stanza windows like a posh boutique
in a semitropical desert. Shall I stop the jokes and speak
for the soul? Soul, was she not your fair and final brightness?

Didn't your bodies fit perfectly? Bone to bone, a
miracle of calibration and metre, didn't the shape
of lips, and the small well under her throat,
rhyme easily as my hand fitting under her damp nape?
She fitted the ribs of my body like a boat.

Shoot the end of this now. Let the last line
be an empty lot after work. West Venice changes its gels
for the fade. We become, said Borges, books when we are
    dying.
I died and did not become any book in the city of angels.

A Propertius Quartet

Sextus Propertius saw his charred Cynthia rise
from the fires of a hell whose libidinous tongues speak
the same language world over, and cried to that horrible
        mummer
scarved in inflammable muslin, to the socketed eyes,
the black tree crumbling, "My Cynthia!" This summer,
I simply repeated him. By the sea house, the lark's window
caught with sunrise the twigs of the almond trees.
Black are the hearthstones, and their ashes reek
when the heart is put out. There's the smell of smoke from a
singed dishcloth. Hell starts from one spark.
This morning, around five, in a city on the edge of winter,
I was startled by an incongruous sound, the flame of cockcrow,
a dialect ululating in its bright tongue, the dumb sound
went on defining the slope of a sinuous mountain,
the sound scratched the sky and caught the muslin curtain.
This is the price we pay, Sextus, for the ridges
of shoulder blades under a sheet, for crevices rendered, necks
curled with seraphic hair. The cock cries with the tearing
sound of a sheet and it picks at stitches
with its beak. She paid for it with a lost earring,
she whose first syllable was Sin, as yours was Sex.

In Italy, imagine: Sextus. Shod, over its broken stones
you couldn't walk barefoot, but here your soles, naked,
still feel the noise of its empire's past in the tide-suck.
"You've simply got to see Italy before you die."
Cynthia was saying this to me, half naked in her bed,
and I promised to study more domes for St. Peter's sake.
But, Cynthia, to scan marble busts after yours? Why?
When we're both trying to learn each other's body by heart?
The statues themselves would choose life over Art.
Although the harbour of Castries has never seen Gaudi,
the ferns of flamboyants at twilight are exactly like Claude's.
"I'll take us there," she said, "I have plenty of money."
The breadfruit leaves were darkening outside the white
    window,
the calabashes were quietly going out of their gourds,
the barrack walls were turning as gamboge as Giorgione,
but she aroused me with this. I saw her frail shadow
ripple over frescoes, whispering under great arches
with honey-light caught in the pores of columns; by now
the frogs were beginning to boom from the Pontine marshes,
gondoliers slid past our bedposts with leaning oars,
marine light on the ceiling wobbled like sinking palazzos,
but not even for you can your Propertius change places.
I couldn't have the best of both worlds at a cost to those
who have only a Third; my gondolas are canoes.
Her cook scraped an enamel plate clean of white redfish bones.

Fall of empires crumbling into their infernal chasm,
division in families, divorce, slowly collapsing gantries,
rockets whirling in fireballs before the astonished augurs
and the Argus eyes of computers; in bed, where we are
most ourselves, what were they to us, Cynthia? Another spasm,
ascribed to the convulsions of human error,
as a jerking leg lies still. An Afghanistan sentry's.
I grew idle as Antony unbuckling the leonine light
from one shoulder. I wanted no empire, laurel, no palm
but yours, and I led it to where pleased it best
while horizons were burning; you wanted no other column.
On a damp mound of soft golden fern my cheekbone would
     rest
as the asp with flickering tongue curled in its basket.
Morning came down varnished stairs in a white terry robe
with bare feet, and soon the sea's ring turned red with heat
under bubbling Colombian coffee, and your Propertius
stood on your cool verandah inhaling the open psalm
of the sunrise over the small harbours
and he would have surrendered his verse to all the Caesars,
the phalanxes of stanzas marshalled in exchange for the peace
contained in the cool marble of your outstretched arm.

IV

In the lost realm of August, the month named for our emperor,
the sun, in days when on beaches the wild potato vine
runs crazily over the dunes with thirst, and sand scorches
and crumbles like the massive blocks made of travertine,
and stars burn at night as far as the empire's torches,
as far as these island villas of a schoolboy's Latin,
I could feel the cold coming under a wrought-iron table,
feel the heat in that outstretched arm turning into marble,
when you said, "I have never loved anyone that old."
And, if you can add to that age the age of Augustus,
and the sixteen thousand suns I have seen expire,
in spite of our differences, or whatever it is called,
why has your Propertius, Cynthia, never been happier?
He writes this in the flare of fall, the last of October,
forcing a sail to go farther and farther away from our island,
watching his verses dribble like sand out of your hand;
and he writes in another language, your venerable
Sextus, on bark that is strange, trees whose alphabet rustles
differently, in the silver age of scarred birches,
of limbs scarfed with fire, and signs it Sextus Propertius,
till charred trees stand in white snow like letters on paper.

Menelaus

Wood smoke smudges the sea.
A bonfire lowers its gaze.
Soon the sand is circled with ugly
ash. Well, there were days

when, through her smoke-grey
eyes, I saw the white trash that was
Helen: too worn-out to argue
with her Romany ways.

That gypsy constancy,
wiry and hot, is gone;
firm hill and wavering sea
resettle in the sun.

I would not wish her curse
on any: that necks should spurt,
limbs hacked to driftwood, because
a wave hoists its frilled skirt.

I wade clear, chuckling shallows
without armour now, or cause,
and bend, letting the hollows
of cupped palms salt my scars.

Ten years. Wasted in quarrel
for sea-grey eyes. A whore's.
Under me, crusted in coral,
towers pass, and a small sea-horse.

God Rest Ye Merry, Gentlemen
Part II

I saw Jesus in the Project.
—RICHARD PRYOR

Every street corner is Christmas Eve
in downtown Newark. The Magi walk
in black overcoats hugging a fifth
of methylated spirits, and hookers hook
nothing from the dark cribs of doorways.
A crazy king breaks a bottle in praise
of Welfare, "I'll kill the motherfucker,"
and for black blocks without work
the sky is full of crystal splinters.

A bus breaks out of the mirage of water,
a hippo in wet streetlights, and grinds on
in smoke; every shadow seems to stagger
under the fiery acids of neon—
wavering like a piss, some l tt rs miss-
ing, extinguished—except for two white
nurses, their vocation made whiter
in darkness. It's two days from elections.

Johannesburg is full of starlit shebeens.
It is anti-American to make such connections.
Think of Newark as Christmas Eve,
when all men are your brothers, even
these; bring peace to us in parcels,
let there be no more broken bottles in heaven
over Newark, let it not shine like spit
on a doorstep, think of the evergreen

apex with the gold star over it
on the Day-Glo bumper sticker a passing car sells.

Daughter of your own Son, Mother and Virgin,
great is the sparkle of the high-rise firmament
in acid puddles, the gold star in store windows,
and the yellow star on the night's moth-eaten sleeve
like the black coat He wore through blade-thin elbows
out of the ghetto into the cattle train
from Warsaw; nowhere is His coming more immanent
than downtown Newark, where three lights believe
the starlit cradle, and the evergreen carols
to the sparrow-child: a black coat-flapping urchin
followed by a white star as a police car patrols.

The Arkansas Testament

(For Michael Harper)

I

Over Fayetteville, Arkansas,
a slope of memorial pines
guards the stone slabs of forces
fallen for the Confederacy
at some point in the Civil War.
The young stones, flat on their backs,
their beards curling like mosses,
have no names; an occasional surge
in the pines mutters their roster
while their centennial siege,
their entrenched metamorphosis
into cones and needles, goes on.
Over Arkansas, they can see
between the swaying cracks
in the pines the blue of the Union,
as the trunks get rustier.

II

It was midwinter. The dusk was
yielding in flashes of metal
from a slowly surrendering sun
on the billboards, storefronts, and signs
along Highway 71,
then on the brass-numbered doors
of my $17.50 motel,
and the slab of my cold key.
Jet-lagged and travel-gritty,

I fell back on the double bed
like Saul under neighing horses
on the highway to Damascus,
and lay still, as Saul does,
till my name re-entered me,
and felt, through the chained door,
dark entering Arkansas.

III

I stared back at the Celotex
ceiling of room 16,
my coat still on, for minutes
as the key warmed my palm—
TV, telephone, maid service,
and a sense of the parking lot
through cinder blocks—homesick
for islands with fringed shores
like the mustard-gold coverlet.
A roach crossed its oceanic
carpet with scurrying oars
to a South that it knew, calm
shallows of crystalline green.
I studied again how glare
dies on a wall, till a complex
neon scribbled its signature.

IV

At the desk, crouched over Mr. _____
I had felt like changing my name
for one beat at the register.
Instead, I'd kept up the game

of pretending whoever I was,
or am, or will be, are the same:
"How'll you pay for this, sir?
Cash or charge?" I missed the
chance of answering, "In kind,
like my colour." But her gaze
was corn-country, her eyes frayed
denim. "American Express."
On a pennant, with snarling tusk,
a razorback charged. A tress
of loose hair lifted like maize
in the lounge's indigo dusk.

v

I dozed off in the early dark
to a smell of detergent pine
and they faded with me: the rug
with its shag, pine-needled floor,
the without-a-calendar wall
now hung with the neon's sign,
no thin-lipped Gideon Bible,
no bed lamp, no magazine,
no bristle-faced fiddler
sawing at "Little Brown Jug,"
or some brochure with a landmark
by which you know Arkansas,
or a mountain spring's white babble,
nothing on a shelf, no shelves;
just a smudge on a wall, the mark
left by two uncoiling selves.

I crucified my coat on one wire
hanger, undressed for bathing,
then saw that other, full-length,
alarmed in the glass coffin
of the bathroom door. Right there,
I decided to stay unshaven,
unsaved, if I found the strength.
Oh, for a day's dirt, unshowered,
no plug for my grovelling razor,
to reek of the natural coward
I am, to make this a place for
disposable shavers as well
as my own disposable people!
On a ridge over Fayetteville,
higher than any steeple,
is a white-hot electric cross.

It burns the back of my mind.
It scorches the skin of night;
as a candle repeats the moment
of being blown out, it remained
when I switched off the ceiling light.
That night I slept like the dead,
or a drunk in the tank, like moss
on a wall, like a lover happier
in the loss of love, like soldiers
under the pines, but, as I dreaded,
rose too early. It was four.
Maybe five. I only guessed
by the watch I always keep

when my own house is at rest.
I opened the motel door.
The hills never turned in their sleep.

VIII

Pyjamas crammed in my jacket,
the bottoms stuffed into trousers
that sagged, I needed my fix—
my 5 a.m. caffeine addiction.
No rooster crew brassily back at
the white-neon crucifix,
and Arkansas smelt as sweet
as a barn door opening. Like horses
in their starlit, metallic sweat,
parked cars grazed in their stalls.
Dawn was fading the houses
to an even Confederate grey.
On the far side of the highway,
a breeze turned the leaves of an aspen
to the First Epistle of Paul's
to the Corinthians.

IX

The asphalt, quiet as a Sabbath,
by municipal sprinklers anointed,
shot its straight and narrow path
in the white, converging arrows
of Highway 71. They pointed
to Florida, as if tired warriors
dropped them on the Trail of Tears,
but nothing stirred in response

except two rabbinical willows
with nicotine beards, and a plaid
jacket Frisbeeing papers
from a bike to silvery lawns,
tires hissing the peace that passeth
understanding under the black elms,
and morning in Nazareth
was Fayetteville's and Jerusalem's.

X

Hugging walls in my tippler's hop—
the jive of shuffling bums,
a beat that comes from the chain—
I waited for a while by the grass
of a urinous wall to let
the revolving red eye on top
of a cruising police car pass.
In an all-night garage I saw
the gums of a toothless sybil
in garage tires, and she said:
STAY BLACK AND INVISIBLE
TO THE SIRENS OF ARKANSAS.
The snakes coiled on the pumps
hissed with their metal mouth:
Your shadow still hurts the South,
like Lee's slowly reversing sword.

XI

There's nothing to understand
in hunger. I watched the shell
of a white sun tapping its yolk

109

on the dark crust of Fayetteville,
and hurried up in my walk
past warming brick to the smell
of hash browns. Abounding light
raced towards me like a mongrel
hoping that it would be caressed
by my cold, roughening hand,
and I prayed that all could be blest
down Highway 71, the grey calm
of the lanes where a lion
lies down on its traffic island,
a post chevroning into a palm.
The world warmed to its work.

XII

But two doors down, a cafeteria
reminded me of my race.
A soak cursed his vinyl table
steadily, not looking up.
A tall black cook setting glazed
pies, a beehive-blond waitress,
lips like a burst strawberry,
and her "Mornin' " like maple syrup.
Four DEERE caps talking deer hunting.
I looked for my own area.
The muttering black decanter
had all I needed; it could sigh for
Sherman's smoking march to Atlanta
or the march to Montgomery.
I was still nothing. A cipher
in its bubbling black zeros, here.

XIII

The self-contempt that it takes
to find my place card among any
of the faces reflected in lakes
of lacquered mahogany
comes easily now. I have laughed
loudest until silence kills
the shoptalk. A fork clicks
on its plate; a cough's rifle shot
shivers the chandeliered room.
A bright arm shakes its manacles.
Every candle-struck face stares into
the ethnic abyss. In the oval
of a silver spoon, the window
bent in a wineglass, the offal
of flattery fed to my craft,
I watch the bright clatter resume.

XIV

I bagged the hot Styrofoam coffee
to the recently repealed law
that any black out after curfew
could be shot dead in Arkansas.
Liberty turns its face; the doctrine
of Aryan light is upheld
as sunrise stirs the lion-
coloured grasses of the veld.
Its seam glints in the mind
of the golden Witwatersrand,
whose clouds froth like a beer stein
in the Boer's sunburnt hand;
the world is flushed with fever.

In some plaid-flannel wood
a buck is roped to a fender—
it is something in their blood.

X V

In a world I saw without end as
one highway with signs, low brown
motels, burger haciendas,
a neat, evangelical town
now pointed through decorous oaks
its calendar comfort—scary
with its simple, God-fearing folks.
Evil was as ordinary
here as good. I kept my word.
This, after all, was the South,
whose plough was still the sword,
its red earth dust in the mouth,
whose grey divisions and dates
swirl in the pine-scented air—
wherever the heart hesitates
that is its true frontier.

X V I

On front porches every weak lamp
went out; on the frame windows
day broadened into the prose
of an average mid-American town.
My metre dropped its limp.
Sunlight flooded Arkansas.
Cold sunshine. I had to draw
my coat tight from the cold, or

1 1 2

suffer the nips of arthritis,
the small arrows that come with age;
the sun began to massage
the needles in the hill's shoulder
with its balsam, but hairs
fall on my collar as I write this
in shorter days, darker years,
more hatred, more racial rage.

XVII

The light, being amber, ignored
the red and green traffic stops,
and, since it had never met me,
went past me without a nod.
It sauntered past the shops,
peered into AUTOMOBILE SALES,
where a serenely revolving Saab
sneered at it. At INDIAN CRAFTS
it regilded the Southern Gothic
sign, climbed one of the trails,
touching leaves as it sent
shadows squirrelling. Its shafts,
like the lasers of angels, went
through the pines guarding each slab
of the Confederate Cemetery,
piercing the dead with the quick.

XVIII

Perhaps in these same pines runs,
with cross ties of bleeding thorns,
the track of the Underground Rail-

road way up into Canada,
and what links the Appalachians
is the tinkle of ankle chains
running north, where history is harder
to bear: the hypocrisy
of clouds with Puritan collars.
Wounds from the Indian wars
cut into the soft plank tables
by the picnic lake, and birches
peel like canoes, and the maple's
leaves tumble like Hessians;
hills froth into dogwood, churches
arrow into the Shawmut sky.

XIX

O lakes of pines and still water,
where the wincing muzzles of deer
make rings that widen the idea
of the state past the calendar!
Does this aging Democracy
remember its log-cabin dream,
the way that a man past fifty
imagines a mountain stream?
The pines huddle in quotas
on the lake's calm water line
that draws across them straight as
the stroke of a fountain pen.
My shadow's scribbled question
on the margin of the street
asks, Will I be a citizen
or an afterthought of the state?

XX

Can I bring a palm to my heart
and sing, with eyes on the pole
whose manuscript banner boasts
of the Union with thirteen stars
crossed out, but is borne by the ghosts
of sheeted hunters who ride
to the fire-white cross of the South?
Can I swear to uphold my art
that I share with them too, or worse,
pretend all is past and curse
from the picket lines of my verse
the concept of Apartheid?
The shadow bends to the will
as our oaths of allegiance bend
to the state. What we know of evil
is that it will never end.

XXI

The original sin is our seed,
and that acorn fans into an oak;
the umbrella of Africa's shade,
despite this democracy's mandates,
still sprouts from a Southern street
that holds grey black men in a stoop,
their flintlock red eyes. We have shared
our passbook's open secret
in the hooded eyes of a cop,
the passerby's unuttered aside,
the gesture involuntary, signs,
the excessively polite remark
that turns an idea to acid

in the gut, and here I felt its
poison infecting the hill pines,
all the way to the top.

XXII

Sir, you urge us to divest
ourselves of all earthly things,
like these camphor cabinets
with their fake-pine coffins;
to empty the drawer of the chest
and look far beyond the hurt
on which a cross looks down,
as light floods this asphalt
car park, like the rush Tower
where Raleigh brushes his shirt
and Villon and his brothers cower
at the shadow of the still knot.
There are things that my craft cannot
wield, and one is power;
and though only old age earns the
right to an abstract noun

XXIII

this, Sir, is my Office,
my Arkansas Testament,
my two cupfuls of Cowardice,
my sure, unshaven Salvation,
my people's predicament.
Bless the increasing bliss
of truck tires over asphalt,
and these stains I cannot remove

from the self-soiled heart. This
noon, some broad-backed maid,
half-Indian perhaps, will smooth
this wheat-coloured double bed,
and afternoon sun will reprint
the bars of a flag whose cloth—
over motel, steeple, and precinct—
must heal the stripes and the scars.

XXIV

I turned on the TV set.
A light, without any noise,
in amber successive stills,
stirred the waves off Narragansett
and the wheat-islanded towns.
I watched its gold bars explode
on the wagon axles of Mormons,
their brows and hunched shoulders set
toward Zion, their wide oxen road
raising dust in the gopher's nostrils;
then a gravelly announcer's voice
was embalming the Black Hills—
it bade the Mojave rejoice,
it switched off the neon rose
of Vegas, and its shafts came to
the huge organ pipes of sequoias,
the Pacific, and *Today*'s news.